Between Here a

SINÉAD MORRISSEY was born in Portadown in 1972 and read English and German at Trinity College, Dublin. In 1990 she received the Patrick Kavanagh Award for Poetry and in 1996 she won an Eric Gregory Award for the manuscript of her first book, *There Was Fire in Vancouver* (Carcanet 1996). She has lived and worked in Japan and New Zealand, but now lives in Northern Ireland. In 1999 she received an award from the Arts Council of Northern Ireland.

'Born in 1972, Sinéad Morrissey is […] a precocious talent whose poems about her stay in Japan are among the anthology's finest. Her techniques – a clear eye for detail and, predominantly, a long line that never quite crumbles into prose – result in an engrossing, intense poetry. Her work shone from Bloodaxe's 1997 *Making for Planet Alice*, and it does again here.'

Stephen Knight, *Metre* (on *New Poetries II*)

'Sinéad Morrissey['s] sequence about Japan must be read by everyone who loves poetry.'

Grey Gowrie, *Daily Telegraph*

Also by Sinéad Morrissey

There Was Fire in Vancouver

SINÉAD MORRISSEY

Between Here and There

CARCANET

First published in 2002 by
Carcanet Press Limited
4th Floor, Conavon Court
12–16 Blackfriars Street
Manchester M3 5BQ

A CIP catalogue record for this book
is available from the British Library
ISBN 1 85754 558 3

The publisher acknowledges financial assistance
from the Arts Council of England

Set in Monotype Bembo by XL Publishing Services, Tiverton
Printed and bound in England by SRP Ltd, Exeter

for Joseph

Acknowledgements

Acknowledgements are due to the editors of the following publications, in which some of these poems have previously appeared: *Blade, College Green, Heat, Landfall, Metre, New Poetries II,* (Carcanet, 1999), *Or Volge L'Anno/ At the Year's Turning: An Anthology of Irish Poets Responding to Leopardi* (Dedalus, 1998), *Poetry Ireland Review, Poetry Review, PN Review, Prop, Span, The Shop, The White Page/ An Bhileog Bhán: Twentieth-Century Irish Women Poets* (Salmon Publishing, 1999), and *Verse.*

'Eileen, her First Communion' was commissioned as part of a series of poems celebrating the art held in the Ulster Museum's permanent collection and was published in *A Conversation Piece* (Abbey Press, 2001). I am very grateful to both the Ulster Museum and to Felix Rosenteil's Widow & Son Ltd. for their kind permission to reproduce 'Eileen, Her First Communion' by Sir John Lavery as the cover painting for this book.

'Goldfish' was published as a broadsheet in a limited edition of 250 copies by Bernard Stone at Turret Books (London, April 1997).

I gratefully acknowledge the receipt of an Eric Gregory Award from the London Society of Authors in 1996, and a bursary from the Arts Council of Northern Ireland in 1999 to help me complete this manuscript.

Contents

Part I

Part II JAPAN

My voice slipped overboard and made it ashore
the day I fished on the Sea of Japan
within sight of a nuclear reactor.

At first I didn't notice,
my flexible throat full of a foreign language
and my attention on the poison of the puffer fish.

★

Sometimes I picture its lonely sojourn
along the coast of Honshu, facing the Chinese frontier.
And then I'll picture its return —

eager, weather-worn, homesick, confessional,
burdened with presents from being away
and bringing me everything under the sun.

PART I

In Belfast

I

Here the seagulls stay in off the Lough all day.
Victoria Regina steering the ship of the City Hall
in this the first and last of her intense provinces,
a ballast of copper and gravitas.

The inhaling shop-fronts exhale the length
and breadth of Royal Avenue, pause,
inhale again. The city is making money
on a weather-mangled Tuesday.

While the house for the Transport Workers' Union
fights the weight of the sky and manages
to stay up, under the Albert Bridge the river
is simmering at low tide and sheeted with silt.

II

I have returned after ten years to a corner
and tell myself it is as real to sleep here
as the twenty other corners I have slept in.
More real, even, with this history's dent and fracture

splitting the atmosphere. And what I have been given
is a delicate unravelling of wishes
that leaves the future unspoken and the past
unencountered and unaccounted for.

This city weaves itself so intimately
it is hard to see, despite the tenacity of the river
and the iron sky; and in its downpour and its vapour I am
as much at home here as I will ever be.

Tourism

Like the relief of markets,
their saffron-coloured cloths and carpets,
purification where two rivers cross, or the widening line of light
entering Newgrange on the winter solstice –

a manufactured prophesy of spring –
the Spanish and the Dutch are landing in airports
and filing out of ships. Our day has come.

They bring us deliverance, restitution,
as we straighten our ties, strengthen our lattés,
polish our teeth. We take them to those streets
they want to see most, at first,

as though it's all over and safe behind bus glass
like a staked African wasp. Unabashedly, this is our splintered city,
and this, the corrugated line between doorstep and headstone.

Next, fearing summary,
we buy them a pint with a Bushmills chaser
and then on to the festering gap in the shipyard
the Titanic made when it sank.

Our talent for holes that are bigger
than the things themselves
resurfaces at Stormont, our weak-kneed parliament,

which, unlike Rome, we gained in a day
and then lost, spectacularly, several days later
in a shower of badly played cards. Another instance, we say,
of our off-beat, headstrong, suicidal charm.

So come, keep coming here.
We'll recklessly set chairs in the streets and pray for the sun.
Diffuse the gene pool, confuse the local kings,

infect us with your radical ideas; be carried here
on a sea breeze from the European superstate
we long to join; bring us new symbols,
a new national flag, a xylophone. Stay.

Eileen, Her First Communion

Years later, after the painting, we planned her wedding.
The dress took days. We cleared the parlour floor
and flooded it with fine, ivory material.
Eileen disappeared. We worked steadily,

stepping carefully over the borders
her body would fill. On the third day my sister
and I raised a dress in her absence
that made her terrified. Too similar,

was all she said. Was it the weight,
we wondered? The colour? But she was back
with the old panic, her desperate familiar.
When the hour came she walked straight

past the saints and up to the altar
without glancing back. Childhood
had turned her neck towards us, once.
At eighteen resolution didn't falter.

A Storm on Jupiter

At the distance from which we photograph
Jupiter's storm is oiling the cloud-flow
over its single eye –
elegance and extremity are shaking hands.

It is the colour of sands set liquid by wind
and the size of all we can touch. We have caught it
four hundred million miles from where we spin,
and stored it. There is a dance here

between the confounding of knowledge
and the building of roads
from the numbers of our imagination
that prove concrete when walked on.

Talent will rise. Whether it comes at once to make a school
in one time and one place, like sickness,
or whether it follows inheritance (a frugal king),
through the single spine of every generation,
as sure as birth, poems will be written.
I've watched this over years of publication.
I cast my nets wide.

Accident, alignment of the stars, or what they've carried with them
from other lives, have made them speak,
condemned to repeat, as from a rubric,
the million poems stored in the memory of language.
Neat as karma, their numbers at any time
are neither less nor in excess of what they've always been.
Cassandra-like, I predict them.

My waters are the English-speaking world.
My nets, publicity.
Their poems flow towards me – tens by the day, hundreds in a week –
and their great gift of sight, which is infectious,
becomes mine to unleash.
Centred in my hands, then, almost everything
that war and travel teach.

Some never retreat once the black ink starts its shape.
Some sculpt for months.
Some, the fortunate ones, are given what they sing
(as compensation for childhood bullying)
unceasingly. They have the queen bee's reproductive energy.
Others sit under a Banyan tree for three days and three nights.
Then bleed what they write.

All see round childhood's corner. Or through puberty's anger,
jealousy's pressure, sex's swagger, mercy's hunger.
They see shadows in the high noon of their lives
when the sun is hot and cocky and controlled.
They feel contamination feed its oil
across their surface and can say, from memory, the colours that occur
when a water source is contaminated.

Nettles

Where you have asked me to follow you is, I imagine,
dark, open to the point of invisibility, and brushed by the invasion
of our honeymoon three years back. You are closing my eyes
with your mouth and your mouth is a warm pool to rest in.

But instead of the night of the beach fire at Bethell's
with its after-dinner moon, dune grasses, sand flies,
cast voices of fishermen, the sense of electrified wonder if we were ever
to lose the other, looms a forest of conquering nettles –

head high, wavering, viscous, sodden,
strangling the loganberries, twining themselves to raspberries,
growing over the bathtub and the bathtub's rainwater –
imprinted on my retina from the day's attempted harvest in the garden.

Street Theatre

They started with sweetness and light,
their faces white as *Mikado* lovers,
their eyes elliptical.
Their ache (a seagull)

was abated (a swan).
Shame was brief –
it came as a bat
hung up in the chest's wall.

It flapped twice in panic,
then slept.
Boredom was a rock that rolled between them.
They ate their dinner off it.

Finally they dealt each other
a deck of disappointments,
snatched them up, flashing,
and swallowed them as swords.

There wasn't an ending proper.
They simply stood back to back
in a frozen unnecessary duel
and waited for coins.

Sea Stones

It is exactly a year today since you slapped me in public.
I took it standing up. You claimed I just ignored it,
that I pretended to be hooked on the dumb-show of a sunset,
splashing, a mile off. Too hooked to register
the sting of your ring finger
as it caught on my mouth and brought my skin with it.

All the next day I rolled with a migraine
down a merciless gallery that was mercifully without sun.
Sloshed tea in the saucer when your name came up.
I couldn't stop the cup of my hurt
flowing over and over until I saw there was no end of it
and only an end to me. How promiscuous pain can be.

He gave me roses. The surprise of butterflies caged in the palms.
And sea stones with tracings of juvenile kisses, scented with risk.
I wrapped them in black at the back of a bottom drawer,
hidden in underwear. The truth – that you never were so vivid
or so huge as the second the street turned towards us
in shock – got dropped between us like a fallen match.

You turned away as the sun disappeared like a ship. And I,
suddenly wanting to be struck again, to keep the fire of your anger lit,
I bit my lip.

& Forgive Us Our Trespasses

Of which the first is love. The sad, unrepeatable fact
that the loves we shouldn't foster burrow faster and linger longer
than sanctioned kinds can. Loves that thrive on absence, on lack
of return, or worse, on harm, are unkillable, Father.
They do not die in us. And you know how we've tried.
Loves nursed, inexplicably, on thoughts of sex,
a return to touched places, a backwards glance, a sigh –
they come back like the tide. They are with us at the terminus
when cancer catches us. They have never been away.
Forgive us the people we love – their dragnet influence.
Those disallowed to us, those who frighten us, those who stay
on uninvited in our lives and every night revisit us.
Accept from us the inappropriate
by which our dreams and daily scenes stay separate.

In Need of a Funeral

Even though no one has died and there is no one
to touch in the coffin the way my brother
touched the dead-man relation
whose name we didn't know, whose features furrowed
like set sugar and whose black nails shone –
I have need of a funeral.

Even though death is not where I wish to go to,
down the wet green road through the straight black gate –
I have love in the morning, a candle, a radio
and a child's smile blooms over my fireplace.
If I don't walk to the river the river is by my window –
I have need of a funeral.

It came to me the day I stole communion in the cathedral,
not knowing what to do and squinting wildly,
that I had need of a funeral.
Something the man said as he tipped wine
and crushed bread felt helpful. He said sometimes a line
between what was and what is can be visible,

which is why we eat flesh and drink blood. *Kirie.*
I took flowers, an Oxfam veil, a bottle of Scotch, a speech
and made it to the sprawl of Milltown Cemetery
where I littered a hill with old shoes and milk teeth.

There was a pattern to the pattern my breath made on the air
as it extended towards the motorway.

M.E.

Like that, Mummy! I've been asking her what it feels like.
Down by the latest tide line, where the sand caves in,
the footprint of an overweight six-foot fisherman,
scouring for bait. Sickness has turned our daughter inside out.

Zero Visibility

That high up, stars hurt like showering flint.
We drove into Flagstaff shell-shocked and vulnerable.
All night the motel light flickered and buzzed,
as in the movie I'd already seen and scripted –
raw and flawless, shot through with falling stars.

The next day was opposite.
Our hands held at arm's length were stolen by fog –
trees, highways and hills were swallowed by distance
and then released again, tantalisingly, slow colour by slow colour.
Exposure was over and we held our breath for them.

By the time we touched the tipped lip of the Canyon
there was nothing to see but breathlessness itself,
its urgent, insisting clouds. You said the earth
was veiling her enormous sex with vapourised tears
and bridal dexterity. If so, I preferred it that way.

I loved the white unrolling river
of her refusal as it stunned us on the banks,
stupid as hit fish, with our cameras and stares.

Rock Pool

These creatures live on faith that the greater sea,
whose roaring pounds and permeates the rock pool's floor,
the rock pool's leather-bound sanctuary, will once again rise up
to the little sea and that their salts will mingle and hold.
My arm submerged is a Eucalyptus tree
in an eighteenth-century birthing room, lurid and luminous.

How the women who have blocked the keyholes
and the door jams with rags and snuffed the candles scurry!
They move as suddenly as the travelling specks of eyes
that haunt vision: one look at them and they're gone
but they still look on. Water pours from the raised fringe
of green gauze like generosity. The pool collects itself again.

These creatures have lodged themselves on the tallest ridge
of the law of averages, the law of probability, and on the memory
of what their ancestors learned and saw, as unswayably
as they swell in crevices and suck rocks. Life flourishes on belief –
it announces quietly how, some day or night, the sea will arrive and save
them

from the starfish-seeking children and evaporation.

How they would shine in a parable on the return of Christ.
How they would give women succour, those who also hang on
for the moon to peak and for water to answer. A stick breaks but does
not break

as it enters the mirror. When I bend to the surface the room underwater
clouds and furrows with breath like a door closing over.
I am not theirs and they will not give me up.

Darwin Man

In the morning the Darwin man stepped out of his bath and went outside.
The sun dished up the shock of a flat world.

In the distance, a mile off, a tree glistened. The tree was taller than
                                                everything.
As tall as a tree in a Nagasaki photograph.

This is known to those who have seen war, thought the man,
who had never seen war.

All night he had knelt in his bathroom because the spinning of the world
                                                had come.
It had the force of a cyclone and the voice of Mars. It was entire.

Weather became a creature, with hands of tides and eyelids of cedar.
Its heart was a windless square of stars.

When he managed to look up, he saw the heart, high over him in the bath,
where there should have been no sky.

So suddenly crystal he thought the storm was over.
Or that everything was over.

A moment as outwitting as when the soul stands up over the body,
and enters silence.

This is governance
ran a thought in part of the man's head left over from grief and fear.

He was sick with reverence
for the speed of all bodily loss, and the toil of the build.

But it was only the eye of the storm passing over –
a glance into abeyance

that shattered sense,
and the creature kept singing.

The Inheriting Meek

Your letter comes with the news that the lake blooms
earlier each year. As yet September is free of it,
but then as though *October* were carcinogenic,
and days could split degrees between them evenly,
the oncogene of the lake turns manic
as soon as the month names change. America storms, the world warms
and a soft algal stretch is beginning its reach
from the shadow of your cabin to the stone-stacked beach.
It shows the time-consuming ambition of the inheriting meek.

You say you lost millennial Christmas in a week
spent injecting the lake with oxygen,
and write a list of the wars you've fought with the dam
so far and lost, that were not as bad as this —
giardia, sabotage, evaporation,
the year of no rain when the lake drained to wrecks,
water skis, exhausted eels, a hub cap off your station wagon,
and Aucklanders brought their children
to stare at the reason for rationing.

This could mean a green, undrinkable eye in the face
of the forest, the irreversible failure of the water supply,
whilst the language of the luminous algae
is murmurous, like intestines, and quaintly victorious.
Stars miss themselves in the eye, but keep their trajectory.
How neat, you say, and mean it, abhorring stasis,
*all change is good. We are piling into a future
we will not escape from easily, if ever,
for we have eaten time.* The algae gather.

Stitches

There has been extravagance in speech
and every spilled, exploded word has been a stitch
in a blanket made for an imaginary baby.
The words went south where the sun was, but stayed hungry.

A name came in the third month. A face followed.
A hair type, a footprint, but the stitches showed.
Imagination's cloth too coarsely woven
for life to catch and cover stitching over.

And then blood. Inevitable, true.
Simple and strong enough to cut all falsehood through.
Later the screen said darkness – no spine, no heart.
And the stitches came apart.

Our Flower Garden

Consider the flowers in our flower garden, how they rot.
Such promising buds! Early and extravagant,
each an answer to the other's colour, each parting lip perfect.
Without warning then, bruised and upset, they let themselves drop.

Into nothingness, an abyss. We watched. Not storms, not frost –
we'd had none. The sun had loved them. Not drought –
we'd watered them. It was a bitterness rubbed them out.
Some wish spoken in moonlight. Some curse.

Such children as these disarm us with their refusal to impress.
How we coax and cry at their withered heads.
But they are resolute. Determined not to touch us
with their possibility, they choose death instead.

Across the hedge the neighbours' poppies soar.
We smile and wave. Behind their backs we roar.

Post Mortem

We found ambition caked around his heart,
    hard as permafrost. Slowly
        we unpacked it, chipping it
block by block into a bucket. It was crude and unforgiving,
    like cement, and came away from the bone
        in white quartz chunks.
He had them fooled. They never guessed in all his airy silence
    how tuned to the pulse of the world he was.
        Arteries were stretched
where his first thirst had widened them, purple
    where the bruises of expansion had formed
        but still, away from the heart stem,
thin. His system pumped ambition till it killed him.

Both kidneys were filled with the by-product of not speaking:
    a viscous residue, yellow where the light had spilled
        into the incision, visibly oxidising.

We found his gifts, variously coloured or stored in variously-
    coloured liquids. His perfect pitch
        a perfect indigo, borrowed from a rainbow,
under an armpit. The lilac sac floating his liver, an impression of peace.
    His third eye lay buried in the pleura of the lungs
        where dreams of the violently deceased
had left their mark in larkspur and magenta. Out of the throat
    we prised a throat stone –
        originally cream, but shaded grey in places
with pain; the stunning span of his vocabulary worn to a solid entity
    by being understated.

He must, at times, have craved amnesia from impressions.
    Meninges cupping the brain were blue –
        the tell-tale print of synesthesia –
and so he tasted shapes, saw orchestral refrains as phantasmagoria,
    but also heard streetlights screaming
        and couldn't sleep in cities. Sir,
the deceased was overly gifted, oppressively bright,
    burdened with experience, psychically aware.
        His silence was the immovable object
the weight of all his talent solidified against. He should be kept
    in a crypt, open to the public, like Lenin is,
        and visited, to prove what sense is.

Jo Gravis in His Metal Garden

Our Lady of Guadalupe appeared to a humble Indian Juan Diego,
and told him to build a church on the Tepayac Hill
but unless he could bring proof the Bishop would not believe Juan Diego
when Juan Diego told Our Lady of Guadalupe
she asked him to hold out his Tilma and there on a cold winter's day
she filled it with the roses of summer
then the Bishop believed Juan Diego and so a beautiful church
was built on Tepayac Hill
it is the most revered place of worship in Mexico
                 – from the wall of a church in Tucson, Arizona

From the window of the midnight-bound Vegas plane
Tucson flares in the desert – a cactus pricked by rain;
lit houses, lit highways and floodlit swimming pools –
a stunned bird in a basin, spreading its wings to cool.
The gaudiness of Winterhaven is visible from air
in the aftermath of Christmas. Down in the dazzle somewhere
Jo Gravis is sleeping in his metal garden. It took a year
of free time strung like stepping stones from hour to hour
to finally clear his yard of rocks and the herbs he grew
as a solitary failed commercial venture – ginseng and feverfew.
Each hour of work an island. As though delivering his heart
from alcohol, he struck down to the bedrock of a humble start
and stood there a long time, exposed and rarified. At first,
he simply let the pictures come, withstood the thirst
and suffered the parade of soldiers, beggars, widows, orphans,
owls without trees and waterless swans and dolphins
until a gate latched in his mind and he had them forever.
He knew then he could commit them to metal to challenge the weather
and started to build. Metal the medium and metal the message,
he turned trolleys into children, knives into rose petals
from the pockets of Juan Diego, miraculous, crimson,
a velvet gift of proof from a virgin in a vision
hardened against the sun. He peeled flesh back from the bone
and fooled no one. When his women with aerial hair were done
his kettle-headed men stood guard against them by a river
of headlights and bicycle wheels. Such honesty in silver
puts constancy in a peeled hand of wires against the sky
and hope in a speechless sort of prophecy –
a teddy bear bound with twine to an orange tree,
its eyes replaced with pearls. With all of these images

hard and permanent and real and safe in cages
Jo Gravis sensed a sweet deliverance, an end to motion,
and finally built himself a wooden bench to sleep on
surrounded by signs – their shadows on his skin a lullaby
to flesh in a fleshless gallery.

This Century, the Next, the Last

My husband requests a sky burial
he wishes to be
as carrion sequestered by leopards
strung up in a desert tree

Back to the familiar corridor he
may choose any opening
but all the rooms contain me
dressed for a wedding

An Anatomy of Smell

It is the easiest part of the day – the ending of it,
here, with you, among sheets that smell of our skin.
I would know your skin in the dark: its smooth magnetic film
would bring me home and cease my being separate
with one blind touch. I know it again now, this expanse
of noise and light between us. It conquers distance.

Hallways of childhood friends had smells, family smells
that followed family members into school as stowaways
in coat sleeves and lunchboxes – slipped giveaways
of origin, of who made who, of what was left to tell
made suddenly clear in every detail as if recently rained on.
One was made of wine; one walked crushed by blankets even under sun;

one carried the antiseptic of insulin packets and coconut dust
about her, in her hair, and later what I knew by force
to be the thin, hard odour of divorce –
shipyard metal caving under sparks, spit, boot polish and rust.
And I knew also that whatever was in my hallway
was exposing the line and the set of my spine like an x-ray.

Now we too have an identity –
the smell of us is through our sheets and wrapped around our home –
invisible ink encoded onto bone.
We have wrought it as surely as any family
forges something wholly themselves and wholly different
and marks each child for life with the hidden nature of their generative act.

From you, the smell of the Tucson desert:
copper deposits, animal skulls, the chalk trajectory
of stars no cloud covers or stains, ochre and chilli.
From me, bog cotton, coal fires, wild garlic, river dirt.
And from the two of us, salt. When we move house
such genealogies as these will follow us.

Home Early

Take off your glasses and see.
He took him at his word. The world blurred
instantly to a Sisters of Charity blackboard.
He was eight years old.
Twenty-four years of adult distance
dissolved to childhood's porous instant

as the contents of his pockets came to mind
the morning he left school
before he should have
sent home with a summer cold.
He remembered the sugared communion wafers
nuns sold in twelves.

Mid-morning heat the whole way home.
Chillies drying in hands. Women extending flour
so far it folded like material, and barrio boys
in their lowrider cars slung out by the drugstore.
A city in abeyance, an in-breath held
until the absence of those in school or work

could be refilled at five.
The feminine underside of days
exposed her wayward, easy stride
and redefined the possible.
The palm tree in his front yard proffered shade.
Before he stepped inside he stooped and paused

on the doorstep, one hand raised.
The street seemed suspended between events –
a tricycle – the youngest child's – abandoned in the driveway;
a branch of the neighbour's olive tree
eternally impeding
a doll's spectacular backward bend.

He thought he'd have his mother to himself.
A day of attention stretched deliciously
through noon and afternoon. No room through all that time
for panic, temper, disarray. When he opened the door
nuns' words floated by uselessly.
Vision failed rapidly.

Lucidity

I

Every night he meets his family, is crumpled with his sisters
in a cellar, or watches as his niece becomes
smaller and smaller until she disappears.

He hides boxes from his mother
that hold the bones of elephants, a warrant for arrest,
the shirts of her own buried father.

Caught either in scenarios of rescue, or with some
bear trap which he's used to trap and kill a man
in Mexico, he knows the man's his brother.

II

Awake, he never phones or writes
and seems so far away in life and mind
from where they are. Amnesia would be kinder –

instead he wants to be a lucid dreamer, to enter
whatever sea of fear and fever
awaits him when he falls. He wants to change the colour

of what's been seen and said, way back,
in the place
he can't remember or forget.

III

Suddenly he wanders, attaching
notes to walls: *am I dreaming? If I meet
my family, then I'm dreaming...*

They cover the house and the whites of his daylight eyes.
Still, every night his family rises
and the smell of harm, the taste of damage

invades him like the rush of a narcotic. He never knows he could escape it
with the thought: *this is a dream, and everything that happens
is a trick...* until he wakes.

IV

*There is an open sky. The kind you find
in desert in November. White clouds go over
at terrible speed. The sky*

*is changing always. There are no ridges
on the land, no corners. At the end
of everything, waving on the ledge*

*of the world, pilots are stumbling to find
their plane. And I am moving backwards, into the source of wind
while they grow*

smaller and smaller until they disappear.

On Waitakere Dam

for Charles Brown

You wanted to up-end the boat
and set it on the lake we lived by
because no one would know.
It was lavish with silverfish and looked
defeated, humped on its secret
like a hand. There was nowhere to go to

but the magnet of the middle lake
where a vapour sat wide as Australia –
as sovereign, as separate, as intimate
with daylight, as ignorant
of clocks and raincoats and boats.
It threw a soft, unwatchable shimmer

we would not be human in.
You dismantled a sky
as you tipped the boat over,
the nest of a possum was robbed.
The hull settled outside-in
as you inverted the universe.

We bobbed in the reeds.
The trees lay down their crowns
beneath us, an underwater canvas
of spectacular women. Above us
the crowds of their branches were cold.
Black swans were nesting in the nesting place,

trees reared to the rim of vision –
we slid on to the centre. At night,
with no lights for miles, the lake
would glitter with the Southern Cross.
It smiled at us
with a million silver teeth.

We'd heard it roar with rain
and watched it coughing eels
over the dam's brim,
too water-sore to keep them any longer.
They fell flinching themselves
into s's or n's.

And now we sat stilled in a boat
in the centre, under the lake's shroud,
and the listening
was for the car of the caretaker –
weaving down from the Nihotipu Dam
with Handel or Bach on the radio.

PART II

Japan

Goldfish

The black fish under the bridge was so long I mistook it
for a goldfish in a Japanese garden the kind the philosophers
wanted about them so much gold underwater to tell them what waited
in another element like breathing water they wanted to go
to the place where closing eyes is to see

I understood the day I closed my eyes in Gifu City I saw Japan
for the first time saw what I had seen the gate to the Nangu
Shrine by the Shinkansen stood straddled before my head and I
held out my hands to touch it and felt changed air it wasn't
there but I walked into it continually and over the gardens full
of pumpkin seeds in the ground and wild red flowers over them they
told me

they brought autumn and they were about my head also in Gifu City all
pearled
in mist and happy as Japanese brides. I saw the JR crates on the night
trains that passed through stations and seemed endless and running
on purpose on time's heels on sheer will to cross Honshu one end
to the other money's own messenger fire down the line. And when you
talked me through

Gifu one end to the other eyes closed I saw what I would never
have seen sighted a transvestite taxi driver set apart on the street
a lost person flowers by the pavement pavements for the blind I saw
music as pulled elastic bands drums as the footprints of exacting gods

I mistook the black fish for an oriental goldfish the flash of gold
on its belly meant it carried its message for the element below it
always one storey down Zen masters attaining one storey down and I,
falling into you, story by story, coming to rest in the place where closing
eyes is to see

Before and After

I

'Agricultural high schools are the worst high schools in Japan.
The kids who swing through locked windows in Junior High
and masturbate in class come here, or ones not retarded

severely enough to merit a home for the disabled,
all teeth and slurred speech nonetheless. They'll leave you notes
to tell you how they're injured in their heads.

A few are sons of farmers come to learn the trade,
but most have come with nowhere else to go.
The children who fall through the sieve of the system

stop falling here for three years. Though if they rape,
or get arrested more than twice, they leave –
a free fall to the bottom, the Yakuza or the sex trade –

we don't follow their sliding through. We're a thin membrane,
the box that holds the anger and the danger from the academic schools,
and the last cradle also. You can't *teach* here –

the children have no notion of oceans or algebra,
they'll want to know the English for sexual positions
and threaten you, perhaps, with aerosols and matches.'

II

I come back from school with baskets of persimmons, flowers
sometimes, a bucket of miso, my head full of people vibrant and broken
somewhere I can't see: all presents I hope I can carry.

At the Agricultural High School near Ogaki City, kindness falls over me
more than anywhere. Like the persimmons in your garden by Yoro Hill –
enough colour in the mouth of winter to stop the cold.

Night Drive in Four Metaphors

I want the woman driving I don't know never to stop
driving us by rice fields on the narrowest roads
that are straight as the line through the kanji for 'centre' –
The eye of an animal skewered and shown on its side.

The smoke from the factories lights up tonight as a gate to a fallen-down
moon.
A moon on its back under the shadow of its circle is a unique moon.
It means home is under the weight of a stone and that brightness can come
from under a shadow –
The whole weight of a cold ball breathing on it and look how it smiles.

The flats for Brazilian factory workers have shirts hung out on balconies
to dry.
The shirts are coloured by game shows and adverts for shampoo.
Full as scarecrows, lines across and lines down of them –
The buildings are ships on a wind sea trying to sail.

And you beside me with your hair overgrown watching the other side
of the world.
Imagine how the stars are split between my window and yours!
The join is unimaginable from under the roof of the car –
Two worlds split open to each other, stars spilling from each.

Between Here and There

No one seems sure of the reason why aprons
are tied to the necks of stone babies in temples.
The priest says 'honour'.
The guide to Kyoto City mentions 'cold
on their journey away from us to the heaven for children'.
I look at them squatting in Buddha-reflection,
wrapped up to the throat in teddy bears and trains.

★

There's a graveyard for miscarriages under Ikeda Mountain
as stark as a bone field. No flowers, tangerines, sake or aprons
but a basin of stone bodies in two parts: square body, round head.
Like oriental soldiers contained by a wall, they would go walking –
spill over with all of the energy for life that fell out of them too soon.
Except that even in stone some bodies have opened –
loose balls in the basin where heads have rolled.

★

Inside the biggest wooden building in the world
sits Japan's greatest Buddha. One hand raised as a stop sign to evil.
The other is flat, flat with comfort and promise, flat enough
for all of us to nuzzle his thumb. His lily flower opened.
His crossing was a falling into light.
Fall with me, he says, *and you'll be raised to the heights
of the roof of the biggest wooden building in the world.*

★

When Nagasawa visits the house of the dead
he leaves at the door his camera and tripod
his champion karaoke voice his miracle foot massage
his classroom dynamics his rockhard atheism
and slips onto the tatami of the prayer room
as the man who can chant any you-name-it soul
between here and Ogaki to paradise.

Nagasawa in Training

Thirty years, say,
since you left your father's temple
for your father's mother temple in Kyoto.

Eight weeks in training. Prayers for the dead
at four in the morning and a lantern over the stairway.
It lit up your face in papery gloom.

From six until eight
you washed four hundred year-old wooden platforms
stopped dead over latticed bamboo

while the sun came over the TV tower
and the colour of the day
began in earnest to upset you.

Lovers lit up in the long grass!
Three hundred and sixty degrees of crashed renegades
all getting up, getting rid of the dew.

You had two broken hearts, a wife
from your father's books awaiting you
and damage, a sense of it, leaking into you.

Before the years came with their appointments, their daughters,
a neighbourhood to pray for and a cancer constituency,
sex was as stark to you

as the room of nothing you were building in your head.
There was nothing to diffuse the light of that morning.
Nothing but moaning and nothing left of you.

Ogaki Festival

They push beer cans into my hands with red and yellow leaves.
I'm so drunk by the fourth lap round the street
that my students who stand to either side have the faces of leaves –

pressed, drained, similar,
falling into a winter future –
and three of them, laughing, hold my head as I cry.

Spring Festival

My body has become the body of the festival:
the vaginas on shrines reduce me to the facts of life.
And my wedding vows to you are this festival's promises –

a roaring in the ears, narrow entrances,
and the two of us hauled into life's own procession
of mother after mother after mother.

Summer Festival

What do you think when you see a mâché vagina
being rammed with a penis as broad as a battering ram
so that children disguised as elements shriek with joy?

You think: *we are disembodied, while the moon herself has a body.*
She is over by the beer stands disguised as a man. One stagger and she'll trigger
the collapse of the dancers. The moon came to watch us and we all fell down.

Autumn Festival

The fields have been sealed with fire. They are singing
the promise of resurrection and revenge. The whole *cho*
scraped of rice and fruit, it is time to go under and store.

In the streets I watch women who are dancing in rings
in the slow, hindered steps of the kimono. Again and again,
a festival of women. They are declaring what's been done.

Winter Festival

They'll padlock themselves with sake against the cold.
They'll bandage their loins. They'll straddle a drum on its side
made from pulled skin and the sign of an upright swastika

and they'll move on a sea of bare men's shoulders, tall as trees,
banging only when the silence has become unendurable.
In the alley there's a pyramid of bright flesh and lanterns, refusing to be born.

To Encourage the Study of Kanji

I've been inside these letters it seems for years, I've drawn them
on paper, palms, steamed mirrors and the side of my face
in my sleep, I've waded in sliced lines and crossed boxes.

They stay, stars in the new-moon sky,
as dead as the names of untraceable constellations.
Intricate, aloof, lonely, abstracted,

some other mind made them and still since then
they've shrunk to a hint at a fairytale. Say I thread beads.
Say I remember a sky of walking pictures.

To Imagine an Alphabet

Too far back to imagine
It all was dissolved
Under soft black strokes
Of a Chinese brush
Diminishing the fatness
Of original things

Animal legs and human legs are emptied of flesh and blood

Patterns from flattened
Ants or a lake drained the facts
That are trees in winter
The spokes of the world went down
In a language that
Went everywhere, stayed put

Put out what you want a woman and man to be the picture will hold
that too

There are stories in skeletons
And after the three fluid
Lines that are Mountain, the four
That are Fire, Ice as a stroke
On the left side of Water –
Problem is Tree in a Box

I hear moaning and see constriction in a picture the colour is cinnamon
the taste is chalk

A mind is inside the lines
All of it and sooner or later
Sex is everywhere, money
Rice fields wives are mostly
Under the roof to like
Is Woman with Child

I get lost in a landscape of noisy ideas that cross and flare in fireworks of
strokes

Like a child who paints a smile
Over signatures makes Yin
And Yang (two kissing fish)
A rising sun in a field
Of wheat I draw windows leaking
On the kanji for Rain

I make my moon round my forest has branches my people are walking
                                        with arms and a head

And then murder comes, a second
Killing, so softly I'm deaf
At the second of entrance.
My pictures defy the eyes.
I see Lamentation as five falling stars,
Grief abroad and walking,

And a terrible stag, flames shooting from his heart, as he prepares to
                                        walk and preach.

February

for Kerry Hardie

There is no kindness in me here. I ache to be kind, but the weather
makes me worse. I burrow and sneer. I stay small, low, cheap, squander

all signs of the thaw by screwing my eyes. It's easier in the dark.
Defeat is the colour of morning, the grey that engenders the
                                                    honeymoon flats

and the chessboard of rice fields between this block and that.
Each field is marked

for the administering of cement, this month or the next.
I am living in boom, before the door frames are in or the driveways drawn.

The new exit from the station to the south
makes Nagoya spread, calls it out further than one city's insatiable mouth

could dream. Factories chew through a mountain beyond my window
and each time I look at it it's less. In the world before the war

this place was famous, a stopping house for the tired and sore.
There was one road only in Japan, and all who walked it walked through

this town. There are photographs of women in an amber light
stopped dead in their surprise at being captured as the image of a time.

Behind them all, the mountain rises white.
They say it stayed so all winter long, a shut door to the north.

The snow scatters now without it. When all the fields are town,
the mountain stones, it will be spring, and I'll be called on

to be generous. There will be days when fruit trees, like veterans
left standing here and there in pools of shade, will forget about use and
                                                                    bloom.

Pearl

Mother, I made a list of what I think has hit me like the brick
you tossed towards the sky when you were seven,
then stood to watch it fall. Gravity after was never as powerful:
when the brick came down, it took you further than the floor –
further than your street's name, your knitted rabbit jumper,
your wanderlust, your mother's censure, your invisible twin, Charlotte
(who suggested it),
further even than your textbook view of heaven, or the spiders' webs
that laced the yard
like illuminated Ferris Wheels in the fairs you ran away to in your sleep.

★

It made the day a room. And you were in it, above another room. And
then you weren't.
You saw the room through water. Then from underneath. Then as
laughter.
And you were a king's daughter, a king whose grandfathers you
somehow knew
and when you turned, your own great grandchildren swam into view,
complaining and distressed. Time stretched like falling honey
and you were everywhere, without a body, watching the ends of vision
dissolve
in expanding lines of blood. The things you told the doctor as you held
your head
and came up from under, were amazing, if he could have been amazed.

★

An aeroplane thrown by lightning, a love affair, a woman with Greek
hair, a crab's personality,
an alphabet, a barricaded nation, the spirit of correction, two years at sea.
These are the things that bring me to this country, and just like then
whole days dissolve to distance. And time is simmering liquid. And
space is gelatin.
I hear my father's anger ringing and see the past and future flattened
to landscapes of familiar failure. And faces haunt the mirror. And
questions watch me.

★

There are treasures in the sea. You told me of the pearl you smuggled from the underwater dynasty of kings and queens. I want to see it, finger it, believe it, be amazed.